D1101301

KITCHEN

HACKS*

BY **ANNABEL STAFF**

PORTICO

FIRST PUBLISHED IN THE UNITED KINGDOM IN 2016
BY **PORTICO**
1 GOWER STREET
LONDON
WC1E 6HD

AN IMPRINT OF PAVILION BOOKS COMPANY LTD

COPYRIGHT © ANNABEL STAFF 2016
PHOTOGRAPHY BY **ANNABEL STAFF** ANNABELSTAFF.COM
DESIGN BY **NIC DAVIES** SMARTDESIGNSTUDIO.CO.UK

ALL RIGHTS RESERVED. NO PART OF THIS PUBLICATION MAY BE COPIED,
DISPLAYED, EXTRACTED, REPRODUCED, UTILISED, STORED IN A RETRIEVAL
SYSTEM OR TRANSMITTED IN ANY FORM OR BY ANY MEANS, ELECTRONIC,
MECHANICAL OR OTHERWISE INCLUDING BUT NOT LIMITED TO
PHOTOCOPYING, RECORDING, OR SCANNING WITHOUT THE PRIOR WRITTEN
PERMISSION OF THE PUBLISHERS.

ISBN 978-1-911042-48-8

A CIP CATALOGUE RECORD FOR THIS BOOK IS AVAILABLE FROM
THE BRITISH LIBRARY.

10 9 8 7 6 5 4 3 2 1

REPRODUCTION BY COLOUR DEPTH, UK
PRINTED AND BOUND BY 1010 PRINTING INTERNATIONAL LTD, CHINA

THIS BOOK CAN BE ORDERED DIRECT FROM THE PUBLISHER AT
WWW.PAVILIONBOOKS.COM

TO BRIAN. MY DAD.
FOR INSPIRING ME.
IT'S A BUBBLE-MAKER!
I MISS YOU AND
YOUR RUBBISH JOKES.

STRAW-BERRY

REMOVE THE HULL OF A STRAWBERRY BY POKING A STRAW THROUGH THE CENTRE FROM TIP TO STALK

FLOSS SLICER

SLICE THROUGH SOFT CHEESES AND CAKES USING UNFLAVOURED DENTAL FLOSS

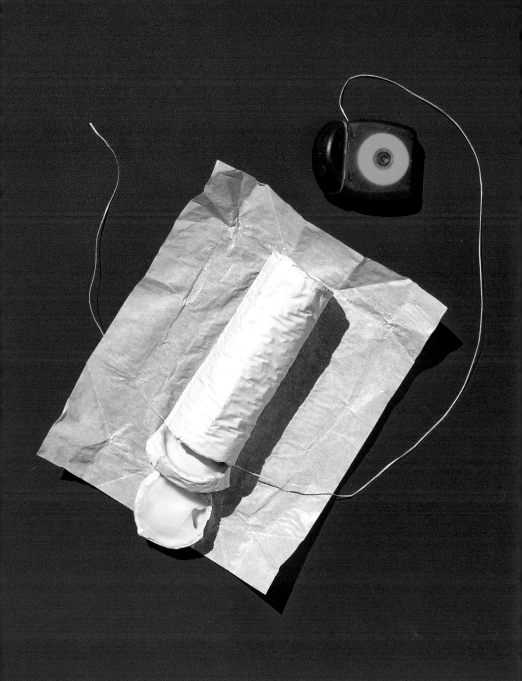

SHELLFISH

EASILY REMOVE STRAY EGGSHELL PIECES BY SCOOPING THEM UP WITH ANOTHER EGGSHELL

ICY HERBS

PRESERVE FRESH HERBS BY FREEZING THEM IN OLIVE OIL, THEN POP CUBES STRAIGHT IN THE PAN WHEN READY TO USE

BUG OFF

STICK A STRAW THROUGH A MUFFIN CASE AND PLACE ON TOP OF SUMMER DRINKS TO KEEP PESKY BUGS OUT

CLIPPED

USE THE CLIP OFF A CHEAP TROUSER HANGER TO SEAL PACKETS OF FOOD

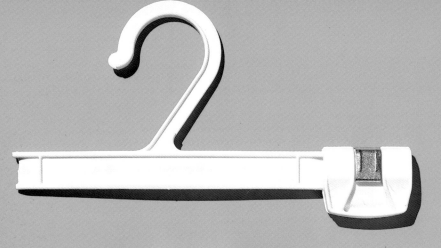

TOP BANANAS

KEEP BANANAS FRESHER FOR LONGER BY STORING THEM SEPARATELY AND WRAPPING THE STEMS IN FOOD WRAP

FRESHLY BAGGED

KEEP A USED TEABAG IN YOUR FRIDGE TO ABSORB ODOURS

AVOHARDO

RIPEN A HARD
AVOCADO FASTER
BY PUTTING IT
INTO A PAPER BAG
WITH A BANANA

CORKED

PLACE CORKS
ON THE TIPS
OF SHARP
KNIVES BEFORE
PUTTING AWAY
IN A DRAWER
TO KEEP YOUR
FINGERS SAFE

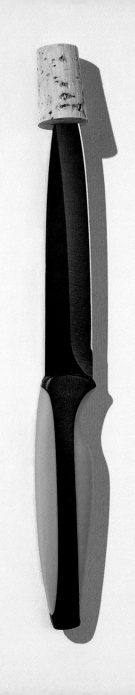

JUICY FRUITS

MICROWAVE LEMONS AND LIMES FOR 10 SECONDS TO GET MORE JUICE OUT OF THEM WHEN THEY'RE SQUEEZED

#12

WRAPPED GREENS

WRAP SALAD GREENS WITH A DRY PAPER TOWEL IN A RESEALABLE BAG SO THEY STAY FRESH IN THE FRIDGE

CHILLY BREAD

FREEZE SLICED BREAD TO KEEP IT FROM GOING MOULDY, JUST POP IT INTO THE TOASTER WHEN YOU WANT TO EAT

14

CAPPED

PUT A SHOWER
CAP ONTO A
BOWL OF FOOD
TO KEEP IT
FRESH

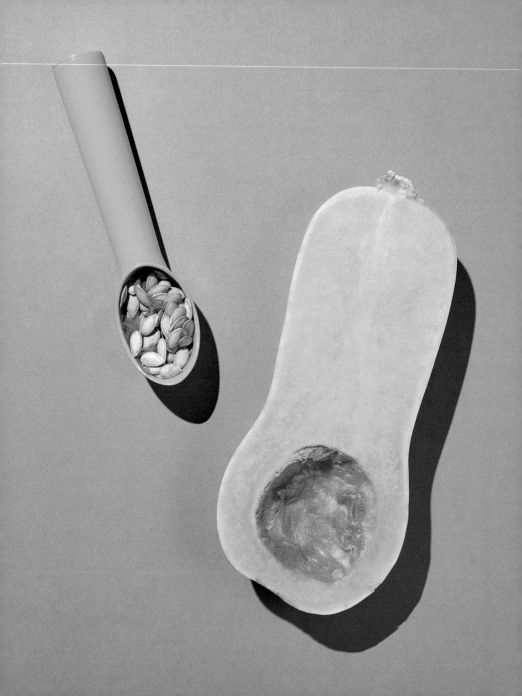

SCOOPED

USE AN ICE CREAM
SCOOP TO DESEED
SQUASHES

RUNNY HONEY

DECRYSTALLIZE HONEY BY SUBMERGING THE SEALED JAR IN A BOWL OF HOT WATER

STEELY AROMA

REMOVE GARLIC AND ONION SMELLS BY RUBBING YOUR HANDS AND FINGERS ON STAINLESS STEEL UNDER RUNNING WATER

SCRUB UP WELL

SCOUR WOODEN CUTTING BOARDS WITH COARSE SEA SALT AND HALF A LEMON, THEN RINSE TO REMOVE INGRAINED DIRT AND SMELLS

BOARDSLIDE

PLACE A DAMP TEA TOWEL BENEATH A CHOPPING BOARD TO STOP IT FROM SLIDING AS YOU CHOP

POP UP

RELEASE THE
SEAL ON A NEW
JAR BY SLOWLY
PULLING THE LID
UPWARDS WITH A
BOTTLE OPENER

English Mustard

Ingredients Water, 24% Mustard Flour, Spirit Vinegar, Sugar, Salt, Mustard Bran, Colour: Curcumin.

Allergy Advice For allergens, see ingredients in bold.

Storage Instructions Store in a cool, dry place. Once opened, keep refrigerated and consume within 6 weeks. Best before end: see lid.

CONDIMENTS, PICKLES & SAUCES · CONDIMENTS, PICKLES & SAUCES

CRACKED & PEELED

ROLL BOILED EGGS ON A HARD SURFACE TO FORM CRACKS THEN SUBMERGE IN COLD WATER TO PEEL EASILY

BUTTERED UP

FLIP A SERRATED KNIFE UPSIDE DOWN TO USE THE FLAT EDGE AS A BUTTER KNIFE

ICED SPONGE

SOAK A CLEAN KITCHEN SPONGE WITH WATER AND FREEZE IN A RESEALABLE BAG TO MAKE A LUNCHBOX ICEPACK

SEED TRAY

SQUEEZE LEMONS OVER A GRATER TO CATCH THE SEEDS

GINGERLY

PEEL GINGER MORE
EFFICIENTLY BY
SCRAPING THE
SKIN OFF WITH THE
EDGE OF A SPOON

FUNNELLED

CUT A LARGE CORNER FROM AN ENVELOPE AND SNIP THE END TO MAKE A FUNNEL FOR DRY INGREDIENTS

ICE WINE

SAVE LEFTOVER WINE BY FREEZING INTO ICE CUBES TO USE IN FUTURE STEWS AND SAUCES

FOAMED

WHISK HOT MILK
WITH A TEA
BALL-STRAINER
TO MAKE A
FOAMY COFFEE
WITHOUT A MILK
FROTHER

SMELLING SALT

PUT SALT IN EMPTY FOOD CONTAINERS TO ABSORB RESIDUAL SMELLS

MARSHMALLOW SUGAR

PREVENT BROWN SUGAR FROM HARDENING BY STORING WITH A MARSHMALLOW